GW00703445

salmonpoetry

*Celebrating 35 Years
of Literary Publishing*

Falling in love
with broken things

Alvy Carragher

Published in 2016 by
Salmon Poetry
Cliffs of Moher, County Clare, Ireland
Website: www.salmonpoetry.com
Email: info@salmonpoetry.com

ISBN 978-1-910669-43-3

COVER ARTWORK: *Lucy Carragher*
COVER DESIGN & TYPESETTING: *Siobhán Hutson*
Printed in Ireland by Sprint Print

*Salmon Poetry gratefully acknowledges the support of
The Arts Council / An Chomhairle Ealaoín*

Dedicated to Lucy, for insisting I write,
and *The Dublin Writers' Forum*, for lighting the way.

Contents

Oranges still make me cry

on summer days
she sliced oranges,
so bitter
they made us cry

wedged in mouths
anchored teeth in
sucked them dry

she gave them to us
fingers clean of juice,
did not take the time
to peel it back
figure out the insides

placed in rows
on the chopping board
held by a ring finger,
as she let the knife
sink into thick skin

they say oranges are
many layered,
clothed, skinned, fleshed

but she knew that
sliced open in wedges
all oranges look the same

Pilgrimage

each year a departure from this yellowing picture
of granny as a dark haired girl, her chin pointed up
towards a sky that does not know its limits yet

each year a step-away from this old photograph,
its curled edges taped down in the front of the album,
she stands, barefoot, half-way up Croagh Patrick

each year another piece of life turned black and white,
still stretching out before this girl, hands on hips,
not knowing time will move like scree beneath her feet

Snapshot

my mother stands almost still, the picture taken
between bouts of Austen and countless nappies,
babies on both hips and exams in the morning,
she has shorn off her hair this time, this photo

hair was just another thing she had no time for,
her eyes, runaway blue, underneath moon glasses,
skin thin, drawn pale beneath her tufty-headed fluff

we are wailing somewhere in the background
it's there in her straining smile,
the can-I-go-now parting of her lips,
she whispered into cradles then, this photo

What she planted

she found us in the dump behind our cottage,
standing up to our knees in rotting cardboard,
tinkering with broken teapots and old dolls

she dug until there was nothing
but wet earth and stones,
planted ivy, roses and clematis,
built low walls to squeeze them into place,
ran her hands along the ridges of fossils,
told stories of lizards trapped in stone

we sucked stalks of rhubarb
that made our eyes wince,
tunnelled through her hedges
to steal blackcurrants,
she cursed blackbirds,
we hid juice-stained hands

we sat on apple tree branches,
craned our necks towards the cottage,
listened to whispers of arguments
and tried not to blame ourselves

when the silence settled,
we always found her
in that place by the trellis,
bent low, pulling weeds,
humming tunelessly
to herself

Christmas morning

peeling brussels sprouts at five a.m. on Christmas morning,
the smell of pine from the tree, turf warming the cool air,
at the kitchen counter with your slippered feet pressed together,
quick wrists as you cut the ends, shucked out the insides

you had been up last to wheel the whiskey breaths to bed
and tuck in our dreams of Santa until morning,
I sat in the dark, heard the kitchen awake and turning

creeping down the spiral of cold stairs, the wet of
the dog's nose against my hand as I felt for the door knob,
your eyes saw past me, sticky still from lack of sleep

I dragged a battered chair across the floor to stand beside you
and in the shiver of the morning took in your sadness,
weighed by the tantrum of greens as each plopped in cold water,
a long list of chores laid out before you, this only the beginning

my head only up to your shoulder, my hand soft from sleep,
took a knife beside you and slower, much slower than before,
we found something peeling sprouts that morning

Our attic

half of Bambi made his way across the lower wall
there was almost enough time to finish the murals,
glitter and grit trapped between floorboards

the small square of a window,
we'd pull the stool under it, scrabble up,
curl into it to watch the seasons go by

that same window, where once my sister
left her pet frog in a lunchbox,
only to find it fried flat later

there was a solid line down the middle,
I'd brush the mess to my sister's side
where it belonged to keep the chaos
from spilling onto me,
occasionally we would switch sides,
spend a day heaving things
across the room, reinvent ourselves,
to inevitably move back again
when rain kept us from other places

a clown hung in the centre of our childhood kingdom
on a swing, his porcelain face jeering,
when I was old enough to reach he disappeared

there was a spiral staircase,
a lethal thing, the stuff of fairy tales,
we'd wheel down the bannister like lunatics
until my brother took a tumble,
and for a week we stepped with care

at night we gripped the top step
hung our heads upside down
to peep downstairs at explicit TV shows,

the horrors of Hannibal Lecter at eight years old,
we spent the night not in, but under, our beds,
whispering Hail Marys and wondered for weeks
about our parents and the things they watched

sometimes we played foxes and rabbits,
constructed tunnels across the room
of bent mattresses and up-turned tables

in time Bambi got blotted out,
and floors refinished, to sell it all off,
but you can't get glitter out of years of grit,
no matter how thick the coat of paint

Timing it

spooning our backs across hay bales,
singing hit me baby one more time,
pointing to clouds, blowing clocks,
smells of hay and black plastic

our rest after the long haul,
knowing the chase was on
once we caught our breath

private concerts and dance-offs
on our curved stage, dangling
out there for all those cows
chewing cuds and flicking flies

we ran at them from fifty metres out,
ground pockmarked from cow hooves,
knocking our wellies off balance

our bodies trundling through air,
we slapped against
their bulking height,
sprawled and insistent,
hands pulling holes in the plastic

I kicked as fast as I could,
fell asleep to summer bales,
damp grass to our knees,
the pelt of our legs in unison,
winning nothing but a downhill,
the sound of our collapse,
at the bottom, into laughter

later, they had me race in fields
with ticker-tape and big clocks
blinking red the time I was taking

now, on lined tracks
I still see your clean heels,
our footstep after footstep,
as we raced across black bales,
flung ourselves over impossible gaps

Confession

he gave me three Hail Marys,
even though I couldn't remember
any sins to tell him and relied solely
on things I'd read in Dennis the Menace,
whispered words I'd heard my parents screaming,
just to hear how they sounded, see his face fall
and figure out how bad they were

I sat in hard pews looking at my sister
bent over in remorse and
wondered if God heard me lying,
stayed head bowed long enough
to look like I'd said mine

I slipped the Hail Marys into my back pocket
and left my sins to sort themselves out

we made our way home,
two miles of country road,
my sister high on forgiveness

I pressed against the cold pane,
our dog cracked against the chain,
there was the smell of scrubbed floors,
the mottle of memories stuck in our carpet

I waited for the slump of my sister through the door,
slower up the last hill home, I had left her there,
the slap of my bag on my back
and from my pocket
the sound of Hail Mary
screaming her own name

the off-kilter crooning of my mother
as she sang eighties music to the oven,
it was easy then,
lost in the ritual of coming home

before the softness broke and the silence fell,
we sat tight fists at the dinner table, waiting
for his words, hoping they landed on someone else

I want to tell my sister, even now,
about the Hail Marys,
how I should have said them for her

Inishturk

I slowed my step for you,
as we dipped between hills,
at the edge of the Atlantic,
they sent us away each morning,
no room in the cottage to hold us,
you tripped to keep up, as we ran
our small wild hearts out to sea

at the cliff's edge,
our backs to the sun,
that big American wind
ripped the coats off our bodies,
we dropped and rolled to keep from blowing over,
cousins told stories of pushing battered cars in,
to watch the sea's snarl swallow them whole

our uncle kept an eye on things,
bent to the window of his front room,
the shake of his sick hands
pressed to the telescope,
waiting for that terrible sea to rise-up
and force out another goodbye

we hid in the calm of the bay,
scrambled over wet rocks and seaweed,
settled to a day spent smashing barnacles,
making bait to fish-out a hundred crabs,
just to throw them back in again,
until, one cracked against a currach,
split its hard shell, and we stood still
as the slosh of water pulled it under,
the dull ring of death sat between us

that night, playing suduko
by the turf fire, huddled together,
and you, too young to understand,
watched my numbers dart across paper,
we walked the black roads,
the sky awake with starlight
led us along pot-holed boreens,
as we counted the wink of houses,
and trusted the land beneath us

The carpenter's daughter

sits in the sawdust heap, because it smells
just like her father, all warm dust and work

sweeps wheelbarrows of it out from under saws,
the scent of steel, the blade still above her head

pulls planks bigger than her across the room,
wants to know how to fix a shelf, or sand a chair

she loves most what wood can become,
rubs the blisters on her soft hands

they'll turn calloused like his carpenter's skin,
a small sacrifice, to be the one, to make-

a new world from that which has fallen,
sliced from the sky to never see it again

she has the gist, but not the knack,
the gist is building with bravery

to take a tree stripped of all its dignity,
then put it back together tenderly

They grow there still

I want to tell his spade hands and flat mind
there are other ways to forget girls like you,
those pale flowers that he left behind

that he walked away, not to be unkind
but because he didn't know what else to do,
I want to tell his spade hands and flat mind

about the trellis where your leaves wind,
how it held you, till you learnt and grew
those pale flowers that he left behind

and if he listened would he learn to find,
the way that you bloomed answers for him too,
I want to tell his spade hands and flat mind

how loving you, makes him soft, not blind
and still those roses grow there, just a few
of those pale flowers that he left behind

but he'd still walk away, even if he knew
the gentle one he'd lose by leaving you,
I want to tell his spade hands and flat mind
about those pale flowers that he left behind

Mother

you said you didn't like the way I wrote you,
it made you feel smaller somehow,
I knew then no pen could spin the words
falling from my eyes to catch you,
I took them out,
all the words I used to show you to myself
and felt the weight of their inadequacy settle
on pages once considered finished

take my hand, let's side step back in history,
smooth out the original birth cert
where you penned with certainty
your own name for me,
it doesn't matter that they later changed it,
I was never anybody else's

you said it was love at first sight
and I know from pictures it was mutual,
blubber cheeks pushed up to scream my laughter back at you

you watched moon-eyed,
wouldn't let them take me from you,
tucked secret wishes underneath my blankets,
woke me from the folds of sleep
to make sure I wasn't hungry for anything

not that we were without our arguments,
the slam of toddler stomps on carpet tiles
when I was exiled for mashing Weetabix into my chair
and later hormones clouded everything in the colours of unfair

if I could go back further
to the times before I knew you,
to the pictures that sometimes scream inside my head
as if there are some kinds of sadness even you cannot contain,

I'd hold your hand there in that shadowy darkness
whisper that it will be ok,
we'll be together soon

I'd follow your trembling footsteps
as you bubble wrapped yourself in old rags
hauling a rusty ladder for a sleigh,
get lost with you in every adventure

curl up beside you,
beg you to read to me in all of your voices,
hide with you in a wardrobe of stories,
build forts from the promises of Austen
and let you know that Mr Darcy
is not the kind of man you wanted to pursue,
listen to your dreams of finding treasure
in ships hidden on the ocean's floor

if we had to press fast-forward,
I'd settle on a rainy Saturday afternoon,
your three girls clustered around
jibber-jabbering questions at you,
collecting moss for badly rendered still lifes
that you still keep hidden in old folders,
our fingers muddy with the licks
of countless batches of banana buns

I'd show you the first poem I wrote
about Poppy, with the sunset spilling from the paper
and let you know that you showed us all the things we do,
made us all the things we are,
taught us that nothing is funny
unless everyone is laughing

the nights you blew ice from your fingertips
so I could chase my dreams,
drove me to the corners of forgotten fields
so I could prove my footsteps matter too

your face broken up in false smiles
at the bottom of that escalator,
loving me enough to let me leave,
both of us knowing I might never come home,
I spent that whole flight crying

you can feel this backbone,
here, you gave to me
the night I thought my heart was broken,
and you held that sodden mess of me,
I wasn't really listening then
but I hear you now and see that there are
always sunsets on other horizons

if I could shutter back in time,
I'd stand a little firmer behind you,
let you know that you will make all the right decisions, eventually,
even if you never get to deep sea dive into old ship ruins

The cactus had an attitude problem

The cactus goaded her with limp prickles
as she sad-eye sashayed through her conservatory –
a greenhouse that poured into the kitchen,
spilling with the scent of obnoxious squashes

you couldn't tell where anything began,
her wicker chairs – a trap for speeches on
the complications of tomato growth in Tipperary,
or sermons on the escape of her tiger worms in 2012,
like the bastard chickens before them,
she had a knack for rearing things,
then letting them go

the cactus failed to show improvement,
its wilted stalk caused her to abandon her principles
of strictly horse manure (she was reared in Offaly)
she became a member of the Miracle Grow Society,
nature left to its own devices would only disappoint

the solution was to be applied liberally,
her cactus multiplied at an alarming rate,
its one bloomed flower like a bruise against the wall,
its savage arms snaked over the coffee canister,
it spread over the cook books – Nigel Slater
and Darina Allen suffered the same fate,
the neighbours started to comment

time saw her feng shui the cactus to the attic
for a stint with the aloe vera,
in hope its temperament would rub off on the stickler,
she stood arm hands around the terracotta pot,
as the cactus attacked,
its prickles clawed their way down her back

it was weeks before the last of the spines were removed,
one would push up under her skin as she sipped coffee
pointing to the clematis steadily eating her trellis,
a hiatus from cacti that leave once they're grown

First kiss

a train station farewell
constructed on an old crate,
an island in our tarmac yard,
we stood at least a person apart

type-cast by myself as a damsel,
I'd seen on one of those saturday morning westerns,
my heart full of smoking guns at seven years old,
I demanded a kiss,
lips sucked inwards, pressed inside gums,
our skin brushed him to a sorry blush,
but I was too busy sprinting after stallions

and that, well that wasn't my first kiss, not really

truth or dare at age eleven
I'd been bullied into books by then,
sitting shelved into Mansfield Park
proving a point to the librarian
who sniffed at the thought,
confused by witty dated intellect

I didn't even note the dare until he sat on top of me
pulled jumper over face and mashed himself
against my mouth, woolly itchy hidden lips

and that, well that wasn't my first kiss, not really

junior cert safely tucked away
all giggles on her bed,
they coaxed me out of Arsenal jerseys into
miniskirts and kitten heels,
blacked out my eyes,
club mecca was more bubbles than brains
and I skirted past preying hands of boyish dreamers

a secret consultation and I was shoved
unsuspecting into the arms of cat-lap tongue,
licking at my mouth like saucer-milk

and that, well that wasn't my first kiss, not really

graduation night, I didn't want to go,
dress fashioned from green silk skirt,
nobody knowing the difference but me,
we'd spent three years avoiding bumping eyes

he grabbed me in a drunken haze,
blatant assault, publicly acceptable
on a teenage dance floor,
he crushed all romantic notions from my mind

and that, well that wasn't my first kiss, not really

oceans from home at just nineteen,
squished up on an armchair
trying not to touch,
watching Fargo on a box tv,
laughing at our best efforts
at Newfoundland twang

it was another week feigning interest in
countless nights of Mario Cart
being subjected to pats on the back,
his idea of a polite goodnight

until, he dipped his finger underneath my chin
and scooped our mouths to where they met,
all my thoughts ran out my toes

and that, well that was my first kiss, really

The night we spilled the holy water

the Virgin Mary knocked sideways on the hall table,
reminded us of our sins, your hands and the floorboards
parachuted us to places older than our years

afterwards, the room smelt like holy water,
we smoked till the cigarettes ran out,
choked on dance steps down Baggot Street
looking for late night liquor and love to drown in

nothing more than our war scars and wet mouths,
on a street paved by glass glint and lamp light,
and we, hoping to be saved, sang heavy to the night

I imagine you saying

she is more than the red dress,
even though it broke up an evening
like nothing mattered but removing it

more than the way she stutters
when she doesn't quite get it

more than deadlines and alarm clocks
and when she's there,
dawn finds you before sleep

more than your shadow breaths
stretching into the half-light

more than a note
that still haunts you,
from a song you didn't recognise

more than the day you found her
dicing vegetables,
eyes wobbling from
something other than onions

more than a mountain side
that stretches out before you,
with a view somewhere
and no easy way to find it

more than song words and dance floors
and drunken waltzing on empty streets

more than a string of metaphors,
than any word you can fit a tongue around
because explaining anything makes it dust

and she is more

It's easier if you pick a moment

one place in time where your eyes met,
most likely there is red wine involved
or mascara and bad but flattering lighting,
there's a dance floor with a pulse
driving you into his arms, remember that

or was there a simpler day,
cocooned in duvets till afternoon,
sunlight filtering your laughter
and he made cinnamon toast
in the sandwich maker,
you got butter in your hair and the bed
smelt like burnt sugar for days

you probably fed each other, at least once,
was it chocolate or grapes or
another excuse to have your
hands bare at the others lips,
mouths salty with the taste of skin

did you catch him, sometimes,
shadowed in the morning,
as he slipped into day-clothes,
you pretended to be sleeping,
so he could leave you a love note
and the coffee seemed sweeter
with his morning words
penned across paper

remember when you sat by water,
head in his lap, just listening,
he told you a story about lost loves
finding their way back to each other,
you didn't think about the words,
just thought that it sounded nice

it's easier if you forget the context,
the fight before, the hours spent
screaming over dirty dishes,
how the bills grew up around you

details will only make you forget,
the part in the story, when he says
he will always love her
and you know with certainty
that he means it

Warning

ask nothing when my hair has lost out to the wind,
the flirtatious bitch of it, cares nothing for me

I've no brush and pucker to hide the bruises,
will always insist we talk about it in the morning
over warmed milk and porridge,
even though nothing irks me like breakfast,
time spent boiling oats to lumpish consistency

it is not just this that scratches at me,
it will be blackbirds cawing against the hours,
traffic lights gone red, the umbrella inside-out
gloves left bedside, cursing puddles, cars,
that two foot tidal wave,
how they've all conspired against me

my mind black and blue with people,
papers to my chest clutching at things to say

leave me to cry silently
over how the spaghetti
is looped in the sink

know none of this is your fault
but I'll blame you anyway,
quiet and insistent as spring rain

Frying eggs

do not whisper to me
ask in return the turnstile of secrets,
I keep this pillow safe for sleeping,
let your hands speak,
turn us over and over,
until we fold in on ourselves
like poached eggs

we will eat, quietly, in the morning,
there is no need for you to sing
as you fry eggs on the old range,
it only heavies my silence

I can't imagine singing an egg
to the sunny-side of anything
and you with your soft, soft dreams,
I want to batter them out of you

Winter mornings

why was it those sharp mornings stung,
as if we'd been slapped too suddenly alive
tucked up, pretending the day had not begun,
we had no jobs or alarms to wake for

your arm weighted across my chest,
holding fast to the last comfort of night,
each waiting for the other to unfurl,
eyes sticky in the damp morning light

we were too far into winter, by then, to fuss
over the way there was nothing left to say,
those dark mornings stood stark before us
and we did not force ourselves to face them

it's clear, now, we'd trespassed into doubt,
each murmuring prayers to keep the cold out

The rain forgets us here

they say it never rains,
not here, not for anyone,
and the weather man confirms it

I've lived my life 'til this
in the quick release
of shower upon shower,
as if time is always grieving

I can't believe the rain will never fall,
as if the sky can't bear to let it go

Not yet

this is one of those casual cafes,
it doesn't trip over its own sentences,
doesn't say too much, too soon,
it offers up little pieces of everything,
hearts on sleeves, vinyl, all the kitsch
mustered onto one distracting wall,
this is where couples curl around coffees
making the smallest talk,
sipping tea from corners of the world,
they've never been to, yet

I keep playing with my jacket,
not sure if I should roll it up or down,
I tug at this chit-chat between us,
not brave enough to ask real questions,
you sit, a comfortable shrug
of jumper and jeans that says
trying, but not really,
I wonder if you'd like my freckles,
hidden in places
you've never been to, yet

do you notice the air between us,
how it is tight with things we want to know,
your last lover and my broken heart,
these things we cannot speak of,
and the light is bright here,
I am tripping over my thoughts
of what any of this means,
and if, this time, I'll end up somewhere
I've never been to, yet

we've both been here before,
not knowing if we will walk out whole,
our hearts still firmly in our chests,
or end up scooped out to places
we've never been to, yet

I want to ask you about Tallahassee

is the apartment as small as ours,
does she cry behind the bathroom door
with the taps turned on
and do you listen

is there an old dirt trail nearby,
does she find her way there,
run till she forgets why
and do you follow

is there a Friday night routine,
does she have you pick the film,
so she can choose the sweets
and do you let her

is the furniture our old sleigh bed,
does she trace the painted flowers
as you hold her at night
and do you love her

After the hurricane

In Galveston, Texas, we saw ruins climb out of water on legs,
they say that before Katrina you could walk out over the sea,
cafes above tides, where you bought trinkets, ate devilled eggs,
fried shrimp or crawfish, stirred lemons through your iced tea

there are shops, still, that sit a little further inland than they used,
bright signs that distract from shaky remnants waving just offshore,
the tourists, no quieter than before, take no note of the abused,
how if you look close enough there's no love in the place anymore

and the locals refuse to board up their windows ever again,
catering instead to the bikinis and buckets that cover the main strip
in "I heart Galveston" memorabilia, hanging off sun-crisped men,
not knowing or caring that ice tea was sweeter before Katrina let rip

locals know that the ghosts of these Texas waters left nothing to save,
their eyes say "Galveston is a dead thing howling over its own grave"

By heart

this kind of love is not new,
it is the shape of my father
lost to his sunday paper,
the sun in the background,
ivy on the white wall, clinging,
and us – we are there –

I still taste the fresh air of a soccer-
ball beating against the sky,
as we try to get him to look up

I've seen this trick before, but no,
I have not figured out its magic,
you are just another man
in the shadow of my father

I see nothing, but stooped shoulders,
how heavy that head must be,
as I tiptoe my hopes after you,
and try to pull you back to me

On letting things go

1

my Grandmother told me that after he died,
it took seven years before she woke without the weight of him

2

they filter in and out,
form a knot in your stomach or a noose in your mind,
it is about loosening the ropes, not forgetting they were there

3

chocolate is a prayer not an answer

4

burning things only makes their stains last longer,
there is nothing left to show the truth of what happened,
do not turn their ashes into myth

5

dance in rain,
feel the endless pelt of this moment,
now, how there is nothing else

6

pictures are a way of haunting yourself with the past,
paper-cutting your heart
with their insistence that this was happy

7

looking over your shoulder will not help you move backwards,
you will only end up stumbling blind into love's next hurdle

8

if you wake with the taste of their name on your lips,
write it down,
do not let them sit at the tip of your mind,
put them away

9

sink to the bottom of something,
open your eyes, let water wash out the screams,
underwater you cannot hear the sound of pain,
only watch its bubbles drift away

10

after seven years, my Grandmother said,
it was more of a dull ache than an open wound

Names she said instead

"Calluna Vulgaris" the word for heather comes easily,
leaning on the gut of a branch, she heaves onwards,
paying homage to names the rest have forgotten

"Rubus idaeus" the plunk of raspberries picked quick,
across the bog, bucket flanking her side,
the berries give her names to say into her son's quiet

"Pomum" safer to hold her kiss to a botched apple
thrown from her orchard's reaching branches,
than think of his lips cold and drained of blood

"Hubert" his name comes heavy with its lack of Latin,
her boy, black and papery with sin, takes her with him

Bedside locker

I've been trying to find ways to tell you mother,
leaving sheets twisted backwards on my bed,
he was everything and nothing like my brother

I broke vases, smashed one against the other,
thinking you would see inside my head,
I've been trying to find ways to tell you mother

there are things I cannot bring myself to utter,
I broke his baby pictures, left them in the shed,
he was everything and nothing like my brother

finger-painting canvas makes me shudder,
knowing places touched like that bleed red,
I've been trying to find ways to tell you mother

I spin dreams upon a star and then another,
but no one hears the things I wish I'd said,
he was everything and nothing like my brother

and every time you say his name I stutter,
hoping you see that parts of me are dead,
I've been trying to find ways to tell you mother,
he was everything and nothing like my brother

Numb

a mouldy old house party, crushed into the dustbin,
as he kissed me, the smell of a dead fish
and I was thinking, this is not ideal, not ideal,
kept glancing over his kisses at a girl in the corner
passed out from space cakes and a dog with cross-eyes
I could have sworn was trying to save me

in the cold room, just upstairs, my hands shivering
in the new moon of a fresh year,
thinking this is not what I resolved,
the burn of whiskey between us
trying to mean something,
and I was thinking, this is not romantic, not romantic,
his hands snatching at me in darkness,
the black of spiders crawling behind my eyelids,
the scrawl of his body pushing me backwards,
and I was thinking, not here, not here

but he didn't know what no means,
didn't know that it was a barrier I was setting up between us,
that it was a wish not to wake four times from my dreams
to his hands and all their nightmares

no meant that it hurt to be drowned in desire,
no was the white of my mind as I shut down
and off until it was all just silence,
'til it was all just movements,
no was my eyes fixed on a ceiling crack
as he moved above me,
hoping it would splinter outwards
and let the stars through

no is a word I've had misunderstood before
by a long term boyfriend
after we first split,

he whispered to me in the
back room of my mother's house
the same thing,
the step too far,
the kind of guy that doesn't know
what no means
afterwards, saying we'll get married,
my heart screaming no, no, no
my heart saying, baby,
you don't know what you've done

I thought it was my fault,
blamed my short skirt,
or my big eyes,
how they were asking for it
under all that mascara

I've heard this same story too many times
most days it's not even mine,
these skeletons of men
that don't know what no means,
we tell each other stories about one night stands
that don't sound like one night stands, laugh-hollow
at things we don't understand, not realising that
the way you said no, it meant something,
even if he never heard you
this is not our fault
no short skirt, or lingerie, or red lipstick
can speak for you

because no means no
and what about the wedge of another word,
beneath your tongue
not sure you should say it,
because it belongs with strangers faces,
and dark alleys and spiked drinks,
rape is a whisper from another girl
a kind of helpless stranger

I kissed both those men goodbye
because I wanted it to be more
than a headache of memory,
more than a dead thing sitting on my chest,
more than the thought of them
criss-crossed and dead-eyed above me,
how it happens again and again and again
more than a girl whose been fucked-over and under,
until she can't remember if she said no,
can't remember if she meant it

Leave me be

do not be distracted by me
I'm a trick played by light or mascara,
there is no space for you here
in these loopholes of arms,
they long to be empty

do not weigh this,
consider it a moment,
it is a slow killing of time,
a blanket tucked over something
that looks lonely

I can't go back there

I thought
I put space between us,
me and your skinny-jeaned soul

the noise of you rung in my ears
long after our last kiss

sidestepped in some street alley,
back boned by cold walls
and warm fingers

the plec we found under the table
resting in beer stains and dust,
I used it to strum away my tears

oh wait, no, that was not me,
I used it to pick the notes of my laughter
as your footsteps receded,
and louder still when you came searching
for things lost in that street alley

you might be looking for me,
so we can have this drama
here, now,
in the quiet places I've been building

Who I'll be for you

I can be the girl in the window,
the half glimpse,
a snatch of dark hair,
eyes that fall away too quickly ,
catching your breath between pale hands
pressed against the panes,
that you won't think about a moment longer

I can be the girl at the bus stop,
somewhere between where you're from
and where you're going to,
with the rain hissing on a country road,
in a bus shelter built for towns
that never settled here
and you imagine getting off for a little while

I can be the girl you pass on an open road,
my footsteps following each other,
eyes fixed on another time
and you think you might double back,
ask what I'm running from
or finding my way back to

I can be the girl on the dance floor,
in a red dress
arms beating to something
more than just music,
smiling when you grab my hand,
lights all around ricocheting our feelings

but I can't be this girl,
this bedtime story,
this morning coffee,
this post-it note on a fridge door
reminding you about eggs
and how much I love you

Mornings

I rise early to see the way light
slowly brushes away the darkness,
how the sky falls into a new day in all its colours
and the stretch of them seems infinite

I rise early to feel the cool of night air,
warming to the kiss of a new day,
and the moon, still hanging in the half-light
wants nothing more than a glimpse of the sun

I rise early to collect salt from rocks,
where the sea licks them by night
but morning sees only the tongue stains
of waves afraid to stay inland any longer

Nights

sea stiller than it's been for days,
palm pressed flat against the sky
willing the yellow belly
of the moon to rise up

I run its edges knowing he'll be there,
impossible to catch the note of melancholy
he presses into the calm,
he only plays to nights like this

the tide caught in and my salty hill
neither dark or light, my footsteps,
his lone voice, hands stuck-cold
to a song he'll play 'til the morning

Canal bank moon walk

I want the sky to be monumental, but it won't cooperate,
better to think about the moon, to stalk the walk of moon talk,
once, you pointed to its round orb, said *it's a mystery for lovers*,
I laughed, but you never meant to be funny

I don't dance like Michael Jackson or know like Kavanagh,
Who would have understood the way you spoke,
always filling each syllable with meaning,
you saw the magnitude in each blade of grass,
those clumps of green hulking with metaphors

I sit on the bench, where you said goodbye,
the place where you first told me your sadness,
we watched a furled swan unravel as if to crack our skulls,
you said something about beauty or transience,
I saw only its hard beak, capable of bone break,
back then, I must have been scared of everything,
fear of swans, mostly, and dying without saying anything

as for the canal, in all its borrowed romance,
you pointed at our trapped reflection,
said *we're stuck in a moment of time*,
and I cursed your brain magic,
I felt nothing, no shimmer, just a watery fish-grave
full of coke cans and slouched condoms

after you left, I started to see others –
doctors, bankers, anyone without a thought for the canal,
I keep their kisses, they don't make me feel insignificant,
they don't know about moonwalking canal banks,
or how you gave me night-time flutters,
they see the dead water that I see,
their scarves are thick and braced for winter,
they all have warm skin, not like,
your cold hand pointing at the moon

Falling in love with broken things

I have been falling in love with broken things
for as long as I can remember,
with ripped jeans or old toys or cakes baked a little sideways

then there is you,
the way we sit cross-legged for hours
leaning into our pasts

yet, I still can't find the thing
that makes your eyes so like those
of a squirrel I found when I was ten,
in a forest thrashed open by storm clouds

waltzing dizzy into my arms,
his eyes full of stories
that I sang back to him,
hoping to hear more
than his breaths narrowing
with the steps back

they said it was just too late to save him

and now, your eyes,
more there than anyone can depend on,
I sing you back my stories

because I have been falling in love with broken things
for as long as I can remember
and I cannot find a way
not to want to save you

In memory of Granny in Galway

on your last night
I stayed away as long as I could,
didn't want another sludge of hours spent counting
hospital tiles or the tip and tap of time passing
as if there was a choice in the matter

the sound of footsteps
trying not to wake the dying,
knowing you too should rest in peace,
away from Granddad who insisted
you looked much better now
and you still slumped and slack-jawed
being drip-fed someone else's dreams

and I imagine, at first, the two of you
stooped over your bent dreams,
how they were black and mangled
dead as your numb foot,
it was only the foot at first,
later the rest went too,
Granddad said every prayer,
lit every candle

he took no notice
when you started to rewind,
you called me 'Sandra',
we did not mention
how you'd forgotten

there are things I will not miss
your wheelchair in the corner, looming,
its two wheels span twenty years of misery
a memory stuck somewhere
between fighting and giving up,
lost in a haze of Coronation Street,
ham-sandwiches and tea

until the pictures they showed us at the funeral
were someone we never met,
standing stick-skinny,
with a jumper to your knees,
hair tossed back in laughter
and we think of your candle
snuffed down to a black wick

we hardly remember you laughing,
just Granddad's cluck of care around you,
missing a beat the day your hand fell heavy
in mashed potatoes,
you sat more red and bloated and determined
than we could bring ourselves to watch
hissing his name, so we wouldn't notice

I didn't want to sit there on your last night,
it was five hours before someone told us it was over,
and you waited till the girls came back
from their cough of fresh air
at 4 a.m. on a summer's night
standing in a hospital car park

we sat by the bed
where you called them angels days before,
a brief moment of recognition
in the catch of a song note on Nancy's throat
as she sang you back to sleep,
I couldn't bring myself to step any closer,
did not trust you'd know my
words from any others

your last night in the hospital bed
the morphine saying you felt nothing,
but your low wail punctuating Lucy's rosary,
the beads clicking quick between her fingers

and when it was over,
when there was no more
fight left in those lungs,
and the leg that gave up long before
wasn't the only part of you without feeling,
when you had forgotten not just me, but everyone

Granddad stood over you saying it didn't seem right,
it didn't seem right, and Daddy clutching your hand
like he could pull you back from that gone place

you might know we lost Granddad too that night,
his hands left empty as he wanders
the halls of your old house,
screaming your name so loud
the neighbours can hear
his last love song

the day we made our way to the funeral,
we found him doing your laundry,
he said he wouldn't be coming
but to remember you well

remember the girl on the island
her hair strapped to the wind
and a heart running faster
than footsteps could carry her,
she who left home at thirteen knowing how to make strong tea
and fish for crabs, with no chance of learning much more,
sent to work away from the slap of sea air

she who walked the streets of Birmingham in a two-piece navy suit
and there wasn't a man didn't stop as she walked by

the young woman she became at the dance hall,
flitting through the hands of young men,
finding granddad in his red plaid suit
and teaching him to smile
one cup of strong tea at a time

the mother that loved her only child like he was the only child,
and how you whispered your first grandchild's name, Alvy,
like a promise

I still think of you,
though I do not visit your grave,
and were I to find my way there
what would I say,
just stand, helpless,
whispering my name to you
over and over

How to wear a white dress

wear a white sundress on a winter's day,
the sort of dress that tosses its hair in beach wind,
that Marilyn would strut across a gutter in,
that requires no underwear,
shows the shimmy in those hips

make sure it is a day
made for blankets and melancholy,
refuse to be either,
say — *I am not a blanket wrapped up in my sadness*,
believe each word, as if it were true

it's important that you take a walk
barefoot, no scarves or gloves,
no umbrellas, or water-proofing,
just you and the dress

you will catch something, not a cold,
although it may be a side effect,
this will be nothing so obvious

the wind will be cutting your skin
until it is pimpled and numb,
but the howling of it will get you

listening to how the birds sing,
between gusts, when they can

seeing how the leaves hang on
and even when they let go
dance downwards, fall softly

standing in rain or hail or snow,
your dress slowly becoming more transparent,
not billowing like the movies would have you believe,
but sticking wet to your thighs

feeling like dancing,
for no reason,
other than you can,
in your white dress
and goose pimpled skin,
the world around you happening

Rain

we were loud as fireworks outside,
huddling our dreams, this time,
we'd be everything, go anywhere

we wouldn't let our hearts be eaten,
still bloody, still raw, from the year before,
wouldn't reel through Temple Bar in blistering heels,
smuggle wine bottles in fur coats to house parties,
drink on the night-link or Dublin bus,
we were never so tacky as our Ribena-filled bottles

there'd be no days spent mending ourselves in the rain
of Dun Laoghaire, out on the pier shivering,
how stupid we were to think rain could fix anything,
no days dredging through charity shops for steals,
or quick cups of tea that spanned hours of moaning
about the same friends kissing the wrong people

this year would be different, I'm sure we laughed,
as we pitched forward and with hands too big
for our damned hearts, thought we'd grab it all

now, we sit with these spaces between us,
the closest we get, my head turned in your
direction, on the edge of the pier, slanting rain,
arms outstretched, finding all things,
however exciting, lead to the same place

Te amo/ Je t'aime/ I love you

smell the beeswax on the dinner table, sister,
muffled quiet, tick of clock hands,
cough out words, try to say the missing thing,
rub the scab on your forehead, your protective moon
hardened around silences you still can't translate,
even now you're grown, a woman

the girl in you hates the ways of the woman
you should have figured it out by now, sister,
sound of knife scratch on plate, you cannot translate,
the secrets of foreign words in your hands,
tongue whispering French under a Spanish moon
and vodka makes words sound like the right thing

scribble your name in the sand, photograph things,
post them online, convince yourself of this woman,
eyes caught sad, smile as big as the moon,
who are you looking at with all that regret, tell me sister,
the next snapshot shows you making gang symbol hands,
thug life and a grin cracked open, for us to translate

haven't seen you in months, easier to translate,
the odd email, filling my inbox with thing after thing,
you theme another party to stop the shake in your hands,
phone to say you feel like the hollow of a woman,
meaning beeswax and childhood, meaning dinner table, sister,
come home, let's yell profanities at the moon

you're a shitbag, fuckwit, calloused old moon,
a sentence anyone can translate,
meaning fuck you moon, you won't eat me alive, sister,
not if you shout back, punch the thing,
rise up against it, I'm asking you, woman,
stop making it worse with the click of your hands

counting Facebook likes, till there's love in your hands,
at night, awake under the bitch of your moon,
it shapes you, makes you this woman,
who says amor and amour as if you can translate
them into words that you understand, the right thing
is to find love in our language, sister

you woman, have amor scratched into your hands,
you, sister, are amour in the light of our childhood's moon,
translating love, yes, love, to find the missing thing

Sisters

it is nine p.m. in Johannesburg,
there is a clear sky in her eye,
the scatter of city lights,
bagpipes sounding up the road,
she sits cross-legged
hanging onto stars and promises
on a window ledge high enough
that nobody can touch her

it is seven p.m. in Tipperary,
the bite of frost in her mouth,
the whisper of country lights,
rusty barns creak into the night,
she runs breathless
counting telephone poles
the stretch of time and land
spread thin beneath her feet

it is six a.m. in Sydney,
the tang of salt water in her nose,
the beat of days beginning,
her arms churn to catch it,
she maps ways to find love,
thinks nothing of drowning
out the slosh of seaweed
and hope beneath her

it is eight pm in Nice,
the sun set slowly in her eyes,
it's been gone now sometime,
but she still sings it sad songs
strapped to her ukulele,
she strums anything other
than the tears that threaten
to take her over

they palm words lettered to each other,
find belonging in postage stamps
and days spent drifting
through hands of strangers

Crab cakes and last suppers

that one night, we sat in her pick-up truck,
the black cloud of trees against night sky,
I cried like a levee had burst in New Orleans

we went to an old crab shack, the fancy kind,
the sort of fancy you only find in Louisiana,
that peppers your mouth with Slap Yo Mamma spices

we ate key-lime pie, or maybe pumpkin,
it didn't count until we'd shoveled in the sugar,
we were doing it the right way, our last-

memory has a way of changing these moments,
its warm air pushing down on grey streets
until it fits the scene of late night Lake Charles

our heads facing forward, her southern lilt,
as we sat in a dark carpark, prolonging
the time left, making it stretch backwards

softening the way we were coming to an end,
there'd be no more liquid cocaine or dance floors
or cakes made from Betty Crocker's box mix

we would not be those girls again,
stuffing their faces, two question marks on a couch,
talking about the boys that made them cry

We never said goodbye

driving past Dublin city
in the almost light of six a.m.
with coffee in our veins
and Oasis telling us
not to look back in anger

the world sliding together
in the slur of morning lights,
promising we'll write or call
a story web across the distance,
knowing we might not find time,
laughing about how you should
really learn to reply to letters

we talk
about things long gone,
easier to speak about
the half mile of boreen
between our house and the main road,
how just before school started back
the hedge was heavy with blackberries,
soft with autumn rain

it's too early
to think of proper things to say,
silence sometimes slips between
the smell of leather seats and wet dog,
you say you won't miss
the dog hairs on your black coat
and I see veins on my hand
as I hold the wheel a little tighter

in the airport everything smells so distant,
and we are the only people
too early to check in,

we try to play cards on plastic chairs,
give up, realising we're only
shortening the minutes

you remind me how you always wanted to go,
even though it's been five minutes now
of staring at strangers,
and you really ought to make your way
to a gate somewhere
or so the intercom tells us

I don't reply,
because there are as many reasons to ask you to stay,
as there are to say goodbye

I walk you as far as they let me,
flustered, you juggle passports,
hands jittery from all that coffee

you say you'll call when you've landed
and that has to be enough, for now

it might be years
before you're back again,
and we'll drive past Dublin city
in the half light of six a.m.
talking about how the time
flew in to meet us

we'll go back to the boreen,
so you can walk that road again,
you'll wear your black coat
and there'll be dog hairs clinging on,
the blackberries will look a little different,
heavier now, from another type of rain

Learning to run (again)

it does not matter, now, that you left me
with my heart jittering to a broken beat,
the buckle of legs that would go no further,
was it out there on some dusty road,
or did you abandon me in a quieter place,
where I could not hear you creep away,
somewhere along a street sluiced in rain,
was I distracted when you upped and left
by the burn of a home-straight on a summer's night,
fighting for seconds on a clock instead of you

it only matters that I find you, now,
waiting in the mornings beyond the house-silence,
I hear you in the dust of laces as the dirt falls off,
the squelching of yesterday's water under foot,
in the crunch of gravel and slap of concrete,
in grass springing back a softer kind of music,
in the muscles stretched out and stretching,
each step takes me closer, each footfall
tracing an old rhythm into new paths,
'til all I have is the sound of you

After the film

hold my hand in an emptying cinema,
as the credits roll in black and white,
it will smell like cold popcorn

someone's song will play,
the one that didn't make the film
most people have left by now,

not us, hand in hand, we'll think
that one person loved it enough
to put it there anyway

I'll think there's love in it,
love, always,
at the bottom of anything

know that happy and sad endings
make me cry the same way,
the credits always come too soon,
leave me questioning everything

Acknowledgements

The first people that must be thanked are my family. To my fellow carpenter's daughters: Mammy, Lucy and Nan. To Lucy – for creating a cover more beautiful than anything I might have imagined and for telling to me write, even when I wouldn't listen; to Mammy – I hope you know that without you none of this would be; to Nancy, my one true bean – for your endless enthusiasm, support and cheerleading; to Peter – for your sensible disinterest in poetry and patience despite it; to Daddy – for giving me the kind of grit, pig-headedness and determination it takes to attempt this; to Ellie – on the day you're old enough to read this, welcome; to Anne – for joining our mad family and making it more, thank you all. Thank you to Stephen Murphy for the endless support and patience.

Thank you to the journals, stages, and festivals that have provided homes for my poems. Special thanks to the following publications for featuring some of these poems: *The Irish Times, Poethead, Skylight 47, The Boheymth, The Doire Press Anthology, The Galway Review, Wordlegs, Ropes, The Pickled Body, Ofi Press Mexico, Poetry Bus* and *Bare Hands Poetry*. Thanks also to the competitions that have listed me, each one was a special moment and I am forever grateful. To Eva Bourke for swinging the door of poetry open and letting me peep in and then writing such kind words to accompany this book, I am forever astounded by your magic. Thanks to Mrs Mary Fahy of Gortanumera National School who was the first teacher to believe in me and encourage me to keep writing.

A big thanks to Colm Keegan for being dead sound (always) and of course your help in finding a publisher. Countless thanks to Anne Tannam for the close attention you gave this collection and the cups of tea, chats about poetry (and more importantly life) and your close edits. To Phil Lynch a poet with a precision for detail that I can only aspire to, thank you for your help with these words. To Aidan Murphy (Mr. Monday Echo) who gave me my first stage and encouraged me despite how terrible the whole thing went, the support you give young writers, poets and musicians is incredible. You should just be thanked constantly. To Jessie Lendennie and Siobhán Hutson and my new family at Salmon Poetry, thank you for making this possible and real. I am forever grateful to the crazy little poetry community – especially *The Dublin Writers' Forum* – where much of this journey began.

A special thank you to Fióna Bolger for your infinite kindness and Liadán for teaching me to be posh (it will come in handy at events). To Kevin Higgins and Susan Millar DuMars for all their support via *Over the Edge*. Thanks to Lisa Frank and John Walsh, at Doire Press, for their encouragement; to Michael Naghten Shanks – for your friendship and support; to Tom Rowley – for videos, stages and being lovely; to Lynn Harding and Ronan Daly – The Fellowship! Thanks to Beau, Tracy and Mart Holland, my Galway family, particularly Beau who sat through many a kitchen rehearsal (my apologies). Thank you, Thekiso for ridiculous energy and sound advice; Ola Kubiak for your endless wisdom. A ridiculously big thank you to my MA family in Galway – many of these poems have been dented into shape by your beady eyes. So here's thanking you Anne Marie Kennedy, Sean Scully, Gemma Creagh, Tommy Hynes, Gloria Snyder, Méabh Browne, Diarmaid Blehein, Keith Bohan, Sarah Miller, Ja McDonagh, Lisa Allen, Martin Keaveney, Ronan (again), you all helped so much. To my other sisters: Cammy, Rachel, Emmylou and Julie – thank you for years of long emails, support and constantly asking to read poems despite their shaky newness. To all the writers, dreamers, friends and family that I have failed to mention. There are too many of you to name, but know you are all here.

ALVY CARRAGHER received a First Class Honours in her MA in Writing from The National University of Ireland Galway, where she focused on poetry. A pushcart nominee, she has been listed for many prizes including: Over the Edge New Writer of the Year, The Gregory O'Donoghue Award, The Cúirt New Writing Prize, Doire Press International Poetry Competition, and the Irish People's Poetry Prize. She is a two-time All-Ireland Slam Poetry Finalist, a Slam Sunday Winner, Connaught Slam Champion and a Cúirt Grand Slam Poetry Champion. In 2016, she was selected for the Poetry Ireland Introduction Series, and was chosen to represent the series at a reading in New York. She has performed at many festivals throughout the country, and even abroad, including: Cúirt International Literary Festival, Edinburgh Fringe Festival, Electric Picnic, Body and Soul, Lingo Spoken Word Festival, and Imagine Waterford Arts Festival. Her poems have featured on RTE's *Arena* on several occasions. Her work has appeared in various publications. She is also an award-winning blogger, and her blog *With All the Finesse of a Badger* has been archived by the National Library of Ireland.